Talking is for

**Raising emotional literacy
in seven to twelve year olds - Key Stage 2**

Dr. Betty K. Rudd

Illustrated by Elizabeth A. Rennison

> **To the loving memory of my mama and papa.**

Published by Lucky Duck Publishing Ltd
3 Thorndale Mews, Clifton, Bristol
BS8 2HX, UK

Commissioned by George Robinson
Book Design by Barbara Maines
Printed in the UK by The Book Factory, Mildmay Avenue, London N1 4RS

© Dr. Betty Rudd 2001
Reprinted April 2002

All rights reserved. No part of this publication may be reproduced, stored in a retrieval system, or transmitted in any form or by any means, electronic, mechanical, photocopying, recording or otherwise, without the prior, written permission of the publisher.

The right of the author to be identified as author of this work has been asserted by her in accordance with the Copyright, Design and Patents Act, 1988.

Foreword

Facilitating good mental health is very rewarding yet it can become an arduous task. It behoves each one of us who is involved in supporting children, whether as a therapist, teacher or parent (of which I am all three), to work out practices and principles enabling the young people to flourish in a healthier way. I hope that this book goes some way towards furthering that enabling process. This book focuses on emotional literacy. A substantial part of this work gives practical suggestions on how to facilitate emotional literacy in individuals aged over seven years and up to twelve. Within this age group, problems can occur because the original emotion has been ignored and remained unprocessed. This book is about the reasons for facilitating emotional literacy as well as how to do this. It does not solve every problem that a child faces, rather, it provides a set of guidelines to use as a yardstick for each child, and a way of solving problems with regard to emotional literacy.

Any person who works with children owes it to these young people, to work as well as they can with them, bearing in mind the budget and other resources which are available. This book contains many practical suggestions and information, both in terms of the written word and in the form of illustrations, to help smooth the path of the facilitator who is enabling emotional literacy in children.

"Talking is for Us – raising emotional literacy in seven to twelve year olds " is the sequel to "Talking is for Kids – Emotional Literacy for Infant School Children" (Key Stage 1). This book is aimed at Key Stage 2, junior school children. It is the second of a planned trilogy. The third book of the trilogy (to be published) "Talking is for Teens – Emotional Literacy for Teenagers" is aimed at young people aged thirteen to nineteen years inclusively. Being involved with children in a healthy way is exciting, but it is much more exciting if that includes being skilled in emotional literacy. Developing emotional literacy can facilitate not only children's mental health but also their physical well being, since the two are inextricably enmeshed. This book helps make that an attainable goal, both by the inexperienced and experienced facilitator alike.

Dr. Betty K. Rudd.
Chartered counselling psychologist, specialist teacher and parent.

Contents

Foreword	3
Chapter 1 What is emotional literacy?	7
Chapter 2 Who says what about emotions?	13
Chapter 3 How are the worksheets used?	17
Chapter 4 Stories, activities and worksheet	25
Chapter 5 Plans for using the Illustrated Story	41
Chapter 6 Photo-copiable worksheets	47
Afterword	74
References	75
Appendix 1 List of useful resources	78
Appendix 2 The emotional curriculum, a developmental approach	80

Acknowledgements

Thank you Barbara and George at Lucky Duck for your interest in this work, your unpressurised support and your patience with me.

Thank you Ursula, for the much appreciated latte and fun when I wanted a break.

Thank you Professor Mary Watts, my doctoral supervisor, for your positive comments about my projects.

Thank you my sister Mary, for being so encouraging about my aspirations.

Thank you my children Sophie, Maria, Ben and Jason, for your vibrant transparency and for altruistically offering to be the first to test out the activities suggested.

Thank you Steve, my husband, for listening, for reading each draft, for all those enriching deliberations, for being there for me.

Chapter 1

What is emotional literacy?

Emotional literacy is the ebb and flow of feeling which links thought and action in life. It is becoming popularly known as 'emotional intelligence' (Goleman, D. 1996). Goleman (1996) declares that emotional intelligence can be taught to children. He states that the following are five principles of emotional intelligence:

1. Knowing what emotion you experience in the present: He considers this as fundamental for insight and self-awareness. *"People with greater certainty about their feelings are better pilots of their lives, having a surer sense of how they really feel about personal decisions from whom to marry to what job to take"* (p 43).

2. Managing the emotions that you experience: He considers this as fundamental for self-care, such as shaking off irritability or gloom. *"People who are poor in this ability are constantly battling feelings of distress, while those who excel in it bounce back far more quickly from life's setbacks and upsets"* (p 43).

3. Being self-motivated: He considers this as fundamental for controlling emotions and delaying gratification in order to be attentive, creative and becoming highly skilled. *"People who have this skill tend to be more highly productive and effective in whatever they undertake"* (p 43).

4. Recognising emotions that others are feeling: He considers this as fundamental for altruism and empathy, which is fuelled by compassion. *"People who are empathic are more attuned to … what others need or want."* (p 43).

5. Coping with relationships: He considers this as fundamental for handling a relationship since much of dealing with relationships is concerned with managing others' emotions; this is underpinned by qualities of

personal impact, popularity and leadership. *"People who excel in these skills do well on anything that relies on interacting smoothly with others, they are social stars"* (p 43-44).

Emotional literacy embraces:
    Zeal
    Self motivation
    Persistence
    Self control.

As opposed to being:
    Mean spirited
    Violent
    Selfish
    Irresponsible.

The key aspects of emotional literacy include emotion or affect (A), action or behaviour (B) and thought or cognition (C). Some emotional literacy programmes are currently being used with children in the United States of America. Those which incorporate A, B and C, are supported by work which states that these aspects are important (see Grant 1992). In the USA, the effective programmes include elements of A, B and C, as listed below:

A (emotional elements)

1. Identify and name emotions
2. Express emotions
3. Assess level of emotions
4. Manage emotions
5. Delay gratification
6. Control impulses
7. Reduce stress
8. Know that behaviour is not the same as emotion.

B (behavioural elements)

1. Verbal: such as asking clearly for what one wants, reacting adequately to being criticised, standing up for oneself, being altruistic, listening non-judgementally to others and being involved in a positive peer group.
2. Non-verbal: having the skills to communicate effectively through body language, vocalising, gesturing, facial expression and eye contact.

C (cognitive elements)

1. Talking to oneself as a way of coping
2. Being aware of one's environment and seeing oneself as part of that environment
3. Having the skills to problem solve such as delaying gratification, finding alternative perspectives and anticipating outcomes
4. Understanding others' viewpoints
5. Knowing what behaviour is proper and what is not
6. Being positive
7. Becoming more aware of oneself.

(Grant, 1992).

It is possible to facilitate the development of emotional literacy in children, using the above facets of A, B and C while encompassing: the awareness of feelings, the expression of emotions, the capacity for honesty, optimism and high self-esteem (see Rudd, 1998). This book is designed to aid in such important facilitation. Emotional literacy is very important because children who are emotionally literate tend to be confident when compared to those who are not (Apter, 1997). Also, individuals who are emotionally literate are healthier than those with less emotional literacy (Baker, 1998). In addition, there is cumulative evidence showing that the mental and physical aspects within people are entwined (e.g. Goleman, 1996; Grant, 1992; Rudd, 1998 and Baker, 1998).

Dr. Chopra (1993) too, declares that emotional attitude and physical health are enmeshed. For example, he states that heart disease is connected to individuals who do not express their anger, have a negative outlook, who have unmanaged stress and do not show their feelings. Yet it is possible to improve the immune system by effectively expressing positive emotions (Goleman, 1996; Baker, 1998; Rudd, 1998 and Chopra, 1993). For instance, laughter decreases stress while boosting the immune system (e.g. Baker, 1998).

It is important to acknowledge the emotions in children, as opposed to not taking any notice of them. The skills that have been shown to be of paramount importance for healthy emotional literacy need to be nurtured. That is why it is important not to ignore them. For instance, life-skills such as helping oneself and obtaining appropriate support, coping with difficulties and valuing oneself are just as important as reading, writing and arithmetic (Schilling, 1996). According to Schilling, the amount of self-awareness one has, the level of compassion one experiences, the level of self-control, the ability to manage anger, make decisions and listen, determines one's strength in emotional literacy.

Schilling (1996) explains that the amygdala within the brain is the centre of the emotional mind and that all information entering the brain is analysed via the amygdala for emotional value before going to the cerebral cortex for processing. *"Data leaving the amygdala carry an emotional charge, which, if sufficiently powerful, can override reasoned thinking and logic"* (p 4). She then goes on to describe the work of the neo-cortex:

"The critical networks on which emotion and feeling rely include not only the limbic system (amygdala), but also the neocortex – specifically the prefrontal lobes, just behind the forehead. This part of the emotional brain is able to control feelings in order to reappraise situations and deal with them more effectively. It functions like the control room for planning and organizing actions toward a goal. When an emotion triggers, within moments the prefrontal lobes analyse possible actions and choose the best alternative" (Schilling, 1996, p 5).

Although all this activity takes place in the brain, it is not usually within one's awareness. Gottman (1998) states that although the rational part of one's mind makes logical connections, the emotional part of the mind takes its beliefs to be absolutely true. That is the reason why it may appear futile when attempting to reason with a person who is emotionally distraught; because reasoning is not in place while feelings are self-justified.

Emotionally literate people are skilled at coping with their emotions, they recognize emotions in others and respond appropriately to them and they are advantaged in their lives because they are happier and more successful in their relationships. Indeed, Schilling (1996) declares that they are also more successful in their careers, when compared with those who are not so emotionally literate.

Importantly: how healthy we are, the way we learn, the way we act and the kind of relationships we have, are all influenced by our emotions. Bearing this in mind, children (and indeed adults) who can satisfactorily cope with their emotions, as well as identify and respond adequately to others' emotions, have an advantage over those who cannot. This advantage extends to various aspects of living such as their interactions with relatives, friends, peers, acquaintances and authority figures. In addition, emotionally literate young people tend to be more content and more likely to be successful in adult life. The following are characteristics of an emotionally literate person compared to one who is not so intelligent with feelings:

- A higher frustration level
- A lower number of fights
- More positive behaviour
- Less loneliness
- Greater health
- Not as easily distracted
- Academic works gets better
- Relationships with others improve
- Self-esteem is higher.

One of the implications of the above characteristics is that both being bullied and bullying, either physically or mentally, is less likely to be actualised with such a psychologically healthy individual. Clearly, the mind has an effect on the body. It is now known that the brain and nervous system communicate with each other and therefore have an effect on the immune system.

Importantly, those chemicals (within our bodies) that send messages to both the immune system and brain are gathered with the most density in the neural sites which manage the emotions. Due to this fact, there are strong implications with regard to health:

- Ignoring emotions renders the immune system less robust.

- Not expressing emotions can lead to increased physical ill health.

- Suppressed anger can be more dangerous than inhaling cigarette smoke.

- Illnesses associated with breathing, such as colds and pneumonia have been linked with being emotionally upset, less than one week before the onset of the illness.

- There is a link between individuals who have caring, loving, emotionally supportive relationships with living longer and recovering from illness much quicker (than those who do not have this kind of relationship).

According to Gottman (1998), the best way of having robust psychological health is to express emotions appropriately, fluidly (i.e. be able to express what is felt emotionally, in verbal terms while keeping others and oneself OK) and have a substantial level of self-awareness. It is therefore argued, that parents, teachers and therapeutic psychological counsellors are emotionally literate themselves so they can be potent role models for any children they care for. Also, that teachers need to have an appropriate emotional literacy programme allotted within the school curriculum, to facilitate their pupils in increasing emotional literacy.

I hope that at least this book goes some way towards the implementation of such a programme. A very useful and fun way I know of propagating emotional literacy in young individuals is by using the co-operative card game that has been specifically designed for such a purpose. (Please see the list of useful resources in Appendix 1.)

Chapter 2

Who says what about emotions?

Emotional literacy is a controversial area and not all have been in favour of it: For example, according to Berne (1964), the creator of Transactional Analysis, people are better off thinking than feeling. However, his view was speculative, as opposed to being based on research. Steiner (1996), one of my emotional literacy teachers and a student of Berne who eventually worked with him, developed the view that being intelligent with emotions was wholesome. Further, Steiner draws upon the research of others to argue his point:

"Lately, experimental psychologists with the aid of sophisticated high-techniques have been able to bring the study of emotions into the scientific fold [National Advisory Mental Health Council, 1995]. The possibility of monitoring minute facial muscle movements, respiration, perspiration, heart rate, brain activity, and other correlates of emotion has resulted in a great deal of research being reported in the literature. Still, as late as 1995, state-of-the-art reviews of scientific emotional research in the American Psychologist offer little usable information in a practical, everyday context" [Lang, 1995; National Advisory Council, 1995] (Steiner, 1996, p 32).

One year before Steiner's above publication, Goleman (1995) offered a rational argument for emotional intelligence. His argument was that one's emotional quotient (EQ) was important because it not only related to one's health, family life and work, but also to how well one did in life, and one's emotional wellness. Not all psychologists took the significance of emotions on board (e.g. Berne, 1970). Others however, encompassed the importance of emotion in their work (see Cassius, 1973; Jacobs, 1973 and James, 1981).

More recent work, as in Rudd (1998) also spotlights the importance of emotion. For instance, McGrellis et al (1998) highlight that young individuals not only wish for material security but also for the giving and taking of love. They state that these youngsters are afraid of being on their own, being unwell, being unemployed and not having a home. Such findings are in line with what many young individuals contemplate in this country, as shown by the research of Swallow and Romick (1998). They also show that children want a sense of power regarding their future.

Martin (1998) offers a convincing argument for a new kind of relationship between the child and the school: A relationship which has the same value as what the child values i.e. relationship as opposed to loneliness. Interestingly, psychologists such as Makin and Ruitenbeck (1998) say that it is important to be in touch with our own psyche and to be active in promoting our health. Those who care for children can nurture psychological well being in the young, which includes emotional literacy. This is exciting. It is exciting because I trust that as the younger generation inherits what we have made of the world, those with good emotional intelligence will keep this world, including themselves, OK. If they do not and they are emotionally intelligent, they will feel uncomfortable and so will then do something about it. Further, they will have the ability to be healthier, more well adjusted and happier (as explained in this book) than if they had not been nurtured to have psychological well being. That is why this is exciting.

It is important to bear in mind that Simons (1998), a Dutch psychologist, declares that teaching and learning are two sides of the same coin. For example, if the teachers decide the goals of learning, then their pupils cannot decide them for themselves; or if the teachers monitor learning, then their pupils will not do it for themselves. Consequently, some learning skills will not develop because practice is needed to monitor learning. Teaching can kill independent learning skills. Interestingly, Simons (1998) has identified how, in Finland, paradoxical tensions have been pinpointed. In particular, he argues that either the way people work together or the culture is preventing desired outcomes.

Under enormous curriculum and assessment pressures, it seems to have been easy to overlook the importance of spotlighting psychological wellness. However, the use of Circle Time in some educational establishments may have started to re-dress the balance.

Obviously, prevention is better than cure. Unfortunately, the cost of common mental disorders in this country is six billion pounds a year (Brown, 1998). Two-thirds of the work force in this country are off work at some time in their lives, mainly due to anxiety or depression. Therefore, lack of education concerning psychological well-being results in a great cost not only to the community, but also to the individual. It is a daunting task to reduce this problem (Brown, 1998). Further, only ten per cent of these individuals are referred to specialists, since the capacity to cater for the other ninety per cent is not available. Brown (1998) argues that a great move is needed towards intervention, with the minimum effort, to help individuals. Carers of children, such as parents, teachers and psychologists, could be key in implementing such a move (Rudd 1998).

Psychological well being has started to be addressed in the classroom, perhaps because it is linked with improved behaviour (see Rudd, 1998; Wallace, 1998 and Robinson and Maines, 1998). In England, Cowie (1998) has helped to pioneer the peer support system in schools to at least counteract violence. Cowie (1998) endeavours to teach communication techniques with the aim of:

- reducing bullying and violence amongst children

- showing ways of teaching in the classroom which create an increased supportive learning environment

- and she is planning to develop a multi-media software pack to decrease bullying and violence in schools.

The growth of peer mediation training for young people (Stacey and Robinson, 1997, and Stacey, 2001) has to be seen as a positive move in encouraging the development of emotional literacy.

A view regarding emotional literacy is offered by Dixon (1998) who thinks that teachers need not only to be listened to but also to be more emotionally literate themselves, so that they can become key in doing something about children who bully. In Japan, the culture is for children to work hard in schools. The education authority in Japan is redesigning the educational curriculum so that the pupils have social skills training and more days off by the year 2002 (Cole, 1998). Interestingly, some have argued that emotional intelligence is not new and that psychologists have known about it for many decades (e.g. Brady et al, 2000). Nevertheless, information on emotional literacy needs to also be available to those outside the field of psychology.

Teachers, for instance, may know about the child's stages of development that Piaget (1929, 1963, 1951, 1932 and 1952) identified; but how many know what EQ is? There seems to be a gap in the literature concerning this issue, and this book goes some way towards filling that gap. Further, a way of assessing the emotional literacy in a child is offered, as well as how to keep a record of that assessment. A record of assessment form can be found on worksheet 1, page 22.

Chapter 3

How are the worksheets used?

The worksheets can be used either independently, or as part of a planned course. If you use the worksheets as part of a curriculum on emotional literacy, you may like to consider making a plan of what your aims are:

- for a session
- for a week
- for a month
- for half a term
- for a term
- and on a yearly basis or more.

You may find some helpful ideas for planning the above in The Emotional Curriculum – A Developmental Progression (Gross et al, 2000), which can be found in Appendix 2.

Both counselling psychologists who have specialised in working with children and educational psychologists can integrate appropriate worksheets into whatever relevant model they choose to use for an individual child or group of children. Parents and teachers can also use the worksheets for their children. In addition, the sheets are self-explanatory and can be used to facilitate children in being creatively occupied in a positive way.

Six key concepts encompassed by emotional literacy are covered, they are:

1. confidence building
2. teaching how to learn
3. moving towards independence
4. social development
5. expressing emotion
6. environmental awareness.

These have been identified as essential by Mortimer (1998). All six of the above contribute to:
    A – affect (emotion)
    B – behaviour (action)
    C – cognition (thinking).

Sometimes these three qualities overlap. The use of A for affect, B for behaviour and C for cognition have been taken from the cognitive behavioural school within the field of psychology.

The foundation upon which this positive programme must be based is the communication from facilitator to child of the following three qualities:

1. Empathy (meaning compassion)
2. Congruence (meaning honesty)
3. Unconditional positive regard (meaning acceptance).
   (Rudd, 1998.)

Individuals interested in developing the three qualities stated immediately above can benefit from taking a basic counselling skills course. A useful contact for this is the Counsellor's Guild (CG) and information on how to get in touch with CG can be found in the list of useful resources in Appendix 1. I also recommend the book Counsellors Basics from CG (see the list of useful resources, Appendix 1).

Each activity sheet in this book contributes to an emotional literacy programme. Since the programme is flexible, you are free to use your imagination and the creativity of the children involved. It is easy to adapt the suggested activities in order for them to be tailor made for a specific child or group of children. Since it is essential to facilitate emotional literacy in a balanced way, it is important to make a plan. When planning an emotional literacy programme, it is important that you to keep in mind the three aspects listed below.

1. Make sure that each one of the six elements listed, are covered by the emotional literacy curriculum:
    confidence
    learning to learn
    independence
    being social
    emotional expression
    environmental awareness.

In this way, you can mark each element on the list as you introduce it to the child(ren).

2. Make sure that you have made enough arrangements so that each individual child can join in. This can be done by photocopying one worksheet per child.

3. Make sure that there is an avenue of communication between the child(ren) and the guardian(s) or parent(s) of the child(ren). This can be ensured by perhaps giving relevant homework, or sending a newsletter to the guardians and parents, or inviting them to a meeting about the activities for teaching and facilitating emotional literacy.

After planning and implementing the emotional literacy curriculum, it is important to assess the programme. You need to decide how much effort you wish to put into this and how much time you have to devote to it. Also, do make a note of the evidence you have with regard to this issue.

If you keep all the evidence you have which supports the emotional literacy curriculum, you can put it on a display. In this way, the children can show off their achievements, both combined and personal. One way of collecting material for a display is to take plenty of photographs, video recordings and audio taped recordings. Collect this material while the children are working on their emotional literacy. Gather material from both individual and group work. Do remember that obtaining such material requires informed consent not only from any child involved, but also from that child's parent or legal guardian. This can eventually accumulate into a body of evidence that could be very useful to monitor progress, evaluate the success of the programme. (I am keenly interested in gathering such evidence for research purposes so I will be most grateful for anything you send me, care of the publisher.)

Assessing can be done at the same time as record keeping. There is a suggested format of how progress can be recorded within every section of an emotional literacy programme. This suggested format also provides the opportunity to assess, so both record keeping and assessing can be done together. You can adapt the suggested format to suit the specific situation your children are in.

The form takes about fifteen minutes to fill in. As a rule of thumb, an assessment record can be gleaned when you first have your group or child, half way through your time with your group or child, and when you finish with your group or child. In fact, each child can record her or his own achievements during these three times. Worksheet 2 can be used for this purpose, by the child and worksheet 1 can be used by the facilitator.

The form in worksheet 1 is suggested as a record of assessment form. It can be photocopied and adapted to suit your particular individual's or children's situation. The list is not exhaustive and is not written in any particular order. It encompasses the following skills:

- Is secure in setting
- Has sense of self worth
- More confident
- Orientates self in environment
- Respects others
- Feels s/he belongs
- Experiences achievement
- Expresses wants and needs
- Listens without interruption
- Honest
- Compassionate
- Can take turns
- Joins group activity
- Plays fairly with children
- Adapts to change
- Works alone for twenty minutes.

The following are the recording worksheets with a model provided for an imaginary child (worksheet 1). A blank format is included in Chapter 6.

Worksheet 2 is an example of how a child can keep a record of their response to a particular activity. All the worksheets can be found in Chapter 6.

Plan for using worksheet 1: Record of assessment

Aim(s): Self-reflection, collaboration, being in touch with personal experience, self-motivation, managing emotion, recognising the feelings of others, coping with relationships.

    Step 1: Ensure that the child has a copy of worksheet 1.

    Step 2: The child tells the facilitator the comments which she or he believes need to go on the sheet.

    Step 3: There is discussion between the facilitator and the child, regarding the above comments.

    Step 4: The comments are mutually decided and either the child or the facilitator fill in the form appropriately.

Worksheet 1 Record of assessment form

Assessment Record	Child's Name: J. Bly	Any other comment: 10 years	
Skills	1ST Date: - 9.9.00.	2ND Date: - 7.1.01.	3RD Date: - 8.5.01.
Is secure in setting	No	Almost	Yes
Has sense of self worth	No	Unsure	Yes
Gaining confidence	Yes	Yes	Yes
Orientates self in environment	No	Sometimes	Yes
Respects others	Yes	Yes	Yes
Feels s/he belongs	No	Occasionally	Frequently
Experiences achievement	Rarely	Sometimes	Usually
Expresses wants and needs	Never	Sporadically	Appropriately
Listens without interruption	Yes	Yes	No
Honest	Don't know	Maybe	Probably
Compassionate	Possibly	Sometimes	Definitely
Takes turn	Yes	Yes	Yes
Joins group activity	No	No	Yes
Plays fairly with other children	Yes	Yes	Yes
Adapts to change	No	With great difficulty	With some difficulty
Works alone for twenty minute	No	Almost	Yes

Plan for using worksheet 2: Record of achievement

Step 1: Ensure that the child has a copy of worksheet 2.

Step 2: Tell the child to read it, starting from the top of the sheet and continuing to the bottom, without filling it in, to obtain an overview of what is needed.

Step 3: Ask the child to fill in the worksheet.

Step 4: With a friend, the child discusses the drawing she or he drew.

Importantly, the worksheets also encompass the following five principles:

1. Knowing the emotion one is currently feeling.

2. Managing the emotions one is experiencing.

3. Being self motivated.

4. Recognising the emotions which others are feeling.

5. Managing relationships.

Each of us is more skilled in one thing and less in another. We are however, able to fill gaps we may have regarding skills in emotional intelligence, and the stories and activities which follow have been aimed at supporting seven to twelve year olds in developing their emotional literacy.

Worksheet 2 Record of achievement

My name: _____

Date I worked on this sheet: _____

It took: _____ minutes to finish it.

I felt: _____ doing it.

This is a drawing of how I felt:

I think that
_____
_____

What I want to do is
_____
_____

Chapter 4

Stories and activities

The following five stories and activities allow you and the children to explore various aspects of emotional development. Story is a safe way for children to explore emotional matters. They will draw on their own experiences but be able to relate these to the characters.

The format is:
- A story
- Follow up questions and activities
- Plan for using the worksheet
- The worksheet.

The worksheets could be used independently without the story and are repeated in Chapter 6.

You can read the story to the children or you might want to photocopy, so they can follow and have a record to make into a booklet along with the activity sheets. You can choose the activities you feel are appropriate for the group and fit into the time available. However many of the activites involve children working and talking together. This is an essential part of this programme and some of these co-operative activites must be included in every session.

Story 1

Cecil and the little creature

Once upon a time there was an old man who had a huge wart on his nose. He was short and skinny, with very wrinkled and baggy skin. He only had one tooth left in his mouth and that was dark brown. The old man looked extremely ugly. His name was Cecil.

One day Cecil felt hungry so he thought that he would quickly go to the shop at the corner of his road to buy some food. In his rush to go shopping, he forgot to lock the door to his bed-sitting room (where he lived). In his bed-sitting room, there was a large cage and inside the cage there was a beautiful tiny animal. Some people said, "That's the most beautiful small animal I've ever seen".

Cecil had found the little animal in the middle of the road, with its tail torn off. He felt sorry for it, knowing that the creature would die if he left it there, so he took it to his bed-sitting room and kindly looked after it. Cecil soon realised that the creature had to be kept in a cage at all times, because it was so vicious. Even though Cecil was good to the animal, it still tried to bite him many times and scratch him viciously with its sharp claws.

While Cecil was out shopping, a ten year old girl was playing with her ball, in the house where Cecil rented a bed-sitting room. The girl's name was Anna. Anna's ball accidentally hit Cecil's door. This made Cecil's door open and Anna thought, "I wonder what's in there?" So she opened the door wide and did something naughty: she went inside.

Anna saw the beautiful little creature and opened the cage door. As soon as that happened, the animal attacked her. The girl had to go to hospital to recover from the attack. When Anna was better and out of hospital, she never went into a stranger's room again. Some people said, "She's learnt her lesson the hard way".

When Cecil returned to his bed-sitting room after going shopping, he felt very sorry that he had left his door open, because of what had happened to Anna. From that day onwards, Cecil remembered to lock his door whenever he went out.

(The originator of this story is Sophie Rudd, aged 11 years.)

Follow-up questions and activities for "Cecil and the little creature":

1. What did Anna do that was wrong?
2. What should Cecil have done before going shopping?
3. Was the little animal good or bad? Why?
4. Was the old man good or bad? Why?
5. Explain the saying, "You can't judge a book by its cover".
6. Find a partner. You think of one good thing and your partner thinks of one bad thing. Make up a story with your partner incorporating one good and one bad thing.
7. Illustrate the story that you and your partner made up (so you each write the same story) then your partner colours it in (so you each do your own illustration for your partner to colour in).

Please note that by facilitating discussions with your children and allowing them to undergo the process of problem solving towards finding solutions to the questions and activities regarding "Cecil and the little creature", you will be aiding them in learning how to find out for themselves as well as supporting them in their social development.

Plan for using worksheet 3: Favourite pet

Aim(s): Environmental awareness and learning to learn.

Step 1: Ensure that the children each have a copy of worksheet 3.

Step 2: Each child thinks about what it would be like if no one took care of them.

Step 3: Ask the children to think about the last time they had something to eat or drink.

Step 4: The children fill in worksheet 3.

Worksheet 3 Favourite pet

How would you feel if you left your room and when you returned you found an injured stranger in it?

_____

_____

Cecil is an old man. How old is the most elderly person that you know?

The oldest person I know is approximately _____ years old.

What should Cecil do before shopping, to stop intruders entering his property?

Cecil should _____

_____

What would your favourite pet be and how would you take care of it?

_____

_____

Draw old Cecil:

This is Cecil

Story 2

Yoko and the bully

Once upon a time there was a girl who was nearly eight years old. Her name was Yoko and English was her second language. She lived in a village in southern England and went to her local village primary school. Yoko was caring towards other individuals. Being a kind girl, she liked to help her teacher.

Abu was a boy in her class. He bullied her by calling her names like "Goody-gum-drops". Occasionally, he poked her with his elbow. Although Abu was a noisy child, it was not easy for him to make good friends. His nick name was, "The School Bully".

One day, while Abu was playing by himself in the school playground, he tripped up and hurt his knee. The fall had torn the skin on his knee and it was bleeding. It hurt so much that he cried big wet tears that rolled down his round cheek. Other children were also in the playground but they passed him by without any help, because they knew that he was a bully. Then Yoko saw him.

Yoko immediately wanted to help Abu. She went over to him and asked someone else to bring a teacher. Together, the teacher and Yoko helped Abu to recover. They gently washed his knee in cold water to clean it and reduce the swelling, then put a plaster on his cut. Yoko and Abu spontaneously started to talk to each other. Yoko said, "Don't worry, you'll be alright".

They became very good friends and Abu stopped bullying Yoko. He liked having a friend that he could talk to and realised that if he stopped bullying and was caring, he could have good friends.

Follow-up questions and activities for "Yoko and the bully":

1. Make up a different ending to the story.
2. How do you think Abu felt when he was hurt and no one came to help him?
3. Find a partner and tell your partner about a time when you helped another person.
4. Listen to your partner as she or he tells you about a time when she or he helped another person.
5. Make a drawing of the person who looks after you most of the time.
6. Let your partner colour in your drawing.
7. Act out the story with your partner.

Please note that by facilitating discussions with your child and allowing them to undergo the process of problem solving towards finding solutions to the questions and activities regarding "Yoko and the bully", you will be aiding them in learning how to find out for themselves as well as supporting them in boosting their confidence and moral development.

Plan for using worksheet 4: Let's talk

Aim(s): For children to know their emotions, manage them, express their feelings, cope with a relationship, be social and experience positive affect (emotion).

Step 1: Ensure that all the children each have a copy of worksheet 4.

Step 2: Ask the children what happens when they feel angry.

Step 3: Ask the children how they feel when they are laughing.

Step 4: Each child works on worksheet 4.

Worksheet 4 Let's talk

Draw a situation that makes you feel good:

Find a partner, talk about your drawing.

Write down what you can do to calm down when you are angry.
_____

_____

With a partner, explain to one another what makes you feel happy, then write down your explanation:

_____

_____

Story 3

The twin

For weeks, Mathew, who was nearly twelve years old, had been going to his drama club. He wanted to be in the yearly play, and be with his friends who were at the club and enjoyed his company. One day, his parents said, "Mathew, we're going to Canada for the whole of your school summer holiday. You know we adopted you when you were three years old? Well, someone called Mark who lives in Canada has contacted us. Mark says that he was adopted when he was twelve weeks old and that he is your biological twin brother. He has tracked down where you live and he wants to meet us all. He wants to meet the whole family".

Mathew felt angry that his parents had decided to take him with them for a long summer holiday, to meet a stranger who said that he was his twin. Mathew shouted, "Oh no! The drama club's doing a play in the summer holiday and I want to be in it. If I go to Canada it means that I can't be in it. I won't see my friends either. How can you do this to me?"

His parents tried to calm him down, saying, "This seems like a chance of a life time. You'll meet someone your own age in Canada, who's longing to meet with you and be a special friend to you. Mathew, it's your twin. You can see your old friends every day at school. Don't worry about the drama club. You'll get a chance to be in a play next year."

Mathew's heart was thumping so hard he thought that it would jump out of his chest. He wanted to scream, "Just do what I want!" He did not scream. Instead of that, he kept quiet and clenched his jaw while frowning. Pouting heavily, he shut himself in his bedroom, feeling that life was unfair towards him.

(I am grateful to Maria, my eldest daughter, for giving me the idea for this story.)

Follow-up stories and activities for "The twin":

1. How do you think Mathew felt about meeting his estranged twin?
2. Find a partner and tell your partner about a time when you did something brave.
3. Describe how you felt.
4. Listen to your partner as she or he tells you about a time when he or she did something brave.
5. After listening to how she or he felt, repeat back to your partner what you have just been told.
6. With your partner, decide on a different ending to Mathew's story.
7. Role-play a happy ending to 'The twin', with your partner.

Please note that by facilitating discussions with your children and allowing them to undergo the process of problem solving towards finding solutions to the questions and activities regarding the story "The twin", you will be aiding them in learning how to find out for themselves as well as supporting them in expressing their emotions and helping their social development.

Plan for using worksheet 5: Recognise feelings

Aim(s): For children to have a sense of self-worth and be happy while working independently and being sensitive to someone else's feelings.

Step 1: Ensure that all children have a copy of worksheet 5.

Step 2: Ask the children to close their eyes and imagine receiving a present.

Step 3: With eyes shut, the children imagine giving a present to someone and seeing that person's response.

Step 4: Fill in worksheet 5.

Worksheet 5 Recognise feelings

Joey gives Gemma a toy she has wanted for a long time. Write down in the box how she feels, then draw the situation before colouring it in.

In the box below, draw a happy situation or use a colour to symbolise happiness.

Story 4

Pollyanna's ninth birthday

Once upon a time there was a girl called Pollyanna. It was her ninth birthday party. Pollyanna's grandfather looked after her. He said that she could have three friends for an afternoon tea party.

The birthday tea consisted of peanut butter sandwiches, pieces of apple, cake and fizzy drinks. Her grandfather put on some music and each of the friends gave Pollyanna a present. She said "Thank you", to each friend, as she took the presents. The friends watched her open them with wide-eyed pleasure.

All the friends were in her class. They were: Yanni, he sat next to her; Sam, she sat at the table next to hers in the classroom and Josephine. Josephine played with Pollyanna every break time at school. All the friends played well together and whenever there was an argument, they always made up afterwards. Each friend was happy when they were all good together.

After the tea party Pollyanna's friends went to their homes and her grandfather gave her a present. It was a purse. She had wanted a purse for a long time and was very happy with it. In fact, it became her favourite object. Each time she looked at it, she experienced a feeling of contentment. She looked at it every day.

Pollyanna was usually very good at getting up in time to go to school in the mornings. Indeed, she was so good at it that she would wake up before her grandfather. One morning, she did not wake up before the grandfather because she had stayed up later than usual to watch the end of a film on the television, the night before. On that morning, her grandfather went into her room to wake her up and noticed that she liked the purse so much, that she slept with it on her bed. This touched her grandfather so much that he put a special note in her lunch box on that day. Pollyanna found it during her lunch-break and read it out loud: "I'm proud of you". She was pleased that her grandfather was proud of her.

Follow-up stories and activities for "Pollyanna's ninth birthday":

1. What is your favourite object?
2. With at least one other person discuss how you would feel, what you would think and do, if you could not find your favourite object.
3. Imagine that Pollyanna's home had been left dirty and untidy after the party. What do you think she and her grandfather would do?
4. On your own, think of all the ways that you can clean and tidy up.
5. If Pollyanna has to cross a road by herself to get to school, what is the safest way for her to cross it?
6. Find a partner. Does your partner agree with the answer you gave to the above question?
7. On a sheet of paper, your partner can draw the grandfather on half of it; you draw Pollyanna on the other half. Co-operate to do this, work together not one at a time.

Please note that by facilitating discussions with your children and allowing them to undergo the process of problem solving towards finding solutions to the story "Pollyanna's ninth birthday", you will be aiding them in learning how to find our for themselves as well as supporting them in environmental awareness and moving towards independence.

Plan for using worksheet 6: The present

Aim(s): Thinking of others, being self-aware, learning to learn and environmental awareness.

Step 1: Ensure that the children each have a copy of worksheet 6.

Step 2: Read through worksheet 6.

Step 3: With partners, the children discuss what they would like to put into worksheet 6.

Step 4: Fill in worksheet 6.

Worksheet 6 The present

Think of someone you love and make a drawing of that person:

If that person gave you a present what would your behavioural response be? - what would you do?

_____

how would you feel?

_____

what would you say?

_____

what would be two inappropriate responses?

_____

_____

Story 5

The school hamster

Fluffy was the name of a hamster that was kept at a junior school. A boy called Aaron was the hamster monitor. That meant that he had to look after the hamster every day at school, before the lessons started.

One day, Aaron was ill and did not go to school. On that day, his teacher had to do extra work at school, because she took care of Fluffy. She did not like doing the extra work and complained to the head-teacher. The head-teacher said, "Leave the problem with me; I'll see to it".

That day, she wrote a letter to every parent whose child went to the school. The letter informed the parents that the school was unable to look after Fluffy and unless the hamster had a new home to go to the vet would kill it. It seemed that no one wanted Fluffy except Aaron. Aaron begged his mum and dad for the hamster and promised to clean its cage, give it food, water and play with it daily.

His parents said firmly, "It's not fair on the hamster. If we get the animal, then we won't be able to go for the weekends away that we're used to because there'd be no one here to take care of Fluffy. That's why you can't have the hamster".

Aaron thought very hard about this. He did not miserably give up his vision of having a hamster. Instead, he thought of his situation as a problem to solve. He thought that perhaps he could quickly destroy the hamster but quickly changed his mind, knowing that that would not only be cruel, but also extremely upsetting. Then he thought that he might steal the hamster and hide it. However, he told himself that this would be a very naughty thing to do and that if he did do that, people would not trust him any more. After all these negative thoughts, he started thinking of positive possibilities. His best idea was to get a friend who lived nearby and loved looking after animals, to take care of Fluffy, whenever he and his parents went away for more than twenty-four hours. Full of hope, Aaron told his parents his best positive idea. His mum and dad stood in silence for what seemed like a long time. At last, they said that Aaron could have Fluffy. He was delighted! The school gave Aaron the hamster. He looked after it every day and when he was not able to, his friend looked after Fluffy. Fluffy lived to a contented and healthy old age.

Follow up questions and activities for "The school hamster":

1. Find a partner. Tell the story of "The school hamster", using your own words.
2. Where do you think you can find information on how to look after a hamster?
3. Make a list of all the things that you do to look after yourself.
4. If your mother was sick in bed and you had to take care of her, what would you think and do?
5. How would you feel?
6. Make a comic strip of the story "The school hamster".
7. Let your partner colour in your comic strip.

Plan for using worksheet 7: Liking and smiling

Aim(s): Practising positive feedback, being able to listen and gain a sense of self-worth.

Step 1: Ensure that all the children have a copy of worksheet 7.

Step 2: Think about what some one might need in order to be healthy.

Step 3: Think about what makes you happy.

Step 4: Fill in worksheet 7.

Worksheet 7 Liking and smiling

Tell someone what you like about them.

Ask someone to explain how she or he feels when smiling; listen to the answer.

Either draw yourself smiling or a shape that represents joy to you:

Chapter 5

The Illustrated Story

Plans for using sheets A - R (in Chapter 6)

About these sheets

These illustrated sheets unfold the story of a junior school child with an emotional problem which is dealt with in a proper manner. It also describes a dream that a young cat has where there is a difficulty which is resolved via mediation. It is a simple yet imaginative story with some sadness which ends happily.

The purpose of the main story is to show that an undesirable situation can be resolved. Although the cat's dream may appear as separate from the story, it is actually linked. This is because there is a parallel process between what happens in the dream and the main story.

Reasons for the alphabetically ordered sheets

The alphabetically marked pages are ordered in such a way that they tell a story in their own right, irrespective of the previous numbered ones. The plans for using these sheets are therefore inserted before the beginning of the story. They are not interspersed between the pages, as they have been for the numbered worksheets earlier. This is because such an action would have broken up the flow of the narrative and illustrations. In this way, it is also easier to photocopy the sheets for the children who will be using them.

Introduction to the story

All children will have experienced both positive and negative emotions, as does the girl in the story. We do not know the reason for the girl's sad state, but we do know that by interacting with a special helper, which includes talking, she gets better. This is the process that the young cat's dream reflects. By reading the narrative, acting it out and talking about it, it may be possible for children not only to relate the situation to a similar experience in their lives - where talking helped them to solve a problem - but also to identify with the emotions of others i.e. the characters in the story. The children can work independently by reading the story individually, to themselves. By letting them read to the end of the story, you will be facilitating them to feel the positive emotion that the outcome of the story ends on.

It is not unusual to discover a solution to a problem during a discussion. That is one reason why being able to express oneself is important. This is a reason why talking is encouraged. Sometimes, changes within the home and school environment can cause behavioural problems. We can only imagine what changes occurred which the girl in the story reacted to by staying in bed and crying. However, relevant support that included talking, enabled her to move in a desired direction (a parallel process happens in the dream).

Plan for using sheets A – R

Aim(s): For children to express themselves in a structured and creative way, to experience positive emotion, work independently and identify with the emotions of others.

Step 1: Prepare sheets A - R into a booklet so that each child has a copy.

Step 2: Children take turns to read aloud the story on the sheets.

2a: First one child reads page A, then the next child reads page B, next another child reads page C and so on, until the whole narrative has been read by the class or group of children who are involved in this activity.

2b: In pairs, one child tells the story to their partner, using their own words to describe what has been read out. (This facilitates a way for children to express themselves creatively yet in a structured way, as does Step 3.) The partner listens. The children who listened, repeat back - using their own words if they wish - what they heard their partners saying. (This facilitates respectful listening towards the first person who created their own words to tell the story which had been read out.) This process can take up a whole lesson or part of a lesson. You decide what is best for your children.

Step 3: The story is acted out, see below. (For this, the class room can be arranged in such a way that there is a 'performance' area and an 'audience' area.)

3a: In groups, the groups simultaneously take about seven minutes to decide how they will act out the story.

3b: Each group's performance can last for approximately three minutes.

3c: The class may watch each group performing, then applaud. (In my experience, this is tremendous fun and the children love doing it.)

Step 4: Each child can make her or his own book about emotions. This step can be follow-on work, perhaps for homework.

4a: Further follow-on work. Colour in the sheets. Take the sheets home to colour in. The children can start this activity in the class if there is time, and any colouring medium can be used (e.g. paint).

Another plan for using sheets A - R

Aim(s): to introduce, recognise and talk about emotions, as experienced by the 'characters' that are in the illustrated story within sheets A - R. (The ideas need not take up a whole lesson. Depending on the ability of the children, the ideas can be used within a term's work and each lesson - or part of a lesson - can focus on one or two [depending on time] of the sheets marked from A - R.)

<u>Idea 1:</u> After reading the story (perhaps you can read it aloud to the children, with feeling so that it rings true, in order to enable them to enter into the world of the story), choose any one sheet (or two consecutive sheets) to photocopy so that each child has a copy of the sheet(s) that you have chosen. The children discuss in groups what might have happened before and after what is on the sheet(s), which is different to the actual story. The groups may each have a different perspective, so a co-operative, fun and friendly way to share the ideas is for each group to role play their ideas to the rest of the class. In this way, it may take a substaintial part of an academic term to work through these sheets.

<u>Idea 2:</u> Activities during the role play can keep the children's interest if they are given the opportunity to role play not only the human characters and animals in the story, but also inanimate objects such as the girl's bedroom door and so on. Then, the child who enacts an inanimate object can be asked imaginative questions such as "As the door of the girl's room, how did you feel when you realised that you were not used very much because the girl just stayed in her bed?" or/ and "How would you have liked the girl to have used you, as the door?" or/and "What do you think the cat could do in the story?" and so on. In this way, the children can think about their acting, about problems and find solutions. They will also be using their imagination while not criticising others, but will be building on the views of others.

Idea 3: In their groups, the children can discuss topics such as "What makes me sad?" and "What can bring happiness?". These and other discussion topics they and you may like to include, can help the children develop their listening skills, understand and recognise emotions and see how they are linked to behaviour.

Plan for using sheet S

Aim(s): For children to have a sense of self-worth, feel secure, keep sight of their own needs and gain confidence.

      Step 1: Ensure that each child has a copy of sheet S.

      Step 2: The facilitator informs the children that although all humans have similarities, each person is also unique and without such uniqueness the world would be a very boring place to live in.

      Step 3: The children discuss, in positive terms, how they are the same and different from one another.

      Step 4: Each child fills in sheet S before it is stapled together to make a booklet incorporating sheets A - S.

Conclusion

Please note that sheets A - S inclusively can be photocopied and stapled together. They then become a booklet that can be used independently of the main book. This is a resource of added value because the children can use it as a simple and positive reading and colouring in booklet. It is one way which reinforces the message that "Talking is for us" communicates.

It has been a tradition to measure logical skills via IQ testing and these have taken priority at least within this state's educational system. Nevertheless, skills to do with emotions are not less important than rational ones. Further, both emotional and rational skills are intertwined within the whole of human intelligence. This book endeavours to offer an emotional literacy curriculum for the junior school years.

Chapter 6

Photo-copiable worksheets

Worksheet 1 Record of assessment form

Assessment Record   **Child's Name:**   **Any other comment:**

Skills   1st Date: -   2nd Date: -   3rd Date: -

Is secure in setting
Has sense of self worth
Gaining confidence
Orientates self in environment
Respects others
Feels s/he belongs
Experiences achievement
Expresses wants and needs
Listens without interruption
Honest
Compassionate
Takes turn
Joins group activity
Plays fairly with other children
Adapts to change
Works alone for twenty minute

Worksheet 2 Record of achievement

My name: _____

Date I worked on this sheet: _____

It took: _____ minutes to finish it.

I felt: _____ doing it.

This is a drawing of how I felt:

I think that
_____
_____

What I want to do is
_____
_____

Worksheet 3 Favourite pet

How would you feel if you left your room and when you returned you found an injured stranger in it?

_____

_____

Cecil is an old man. How old is the most elderly person that you know?

The oldest person I know is approximately ____ years old.

What should Cecil do before shopping, to stop intruders entering his property?

Cecil should _____

_____

What would your favourite pet be and how would you take care of it?

_____

_____

Draw old Cecil:

This is Cecil

Worksheet 4 Let's talk

Draw a situation that makes you feel good:

Find a partner, talk about your drawing.

Write down what you can do to calm down when you are angry.

_____

_____

With a partner, explain to one another what makes you feel happy, then write down your explanation:

_____

_____

Worksheet 5 Recognise feelings

Joey gives Gemma a toy she has wanted for a long time. Write down in the box how she feels, then draw the situation before colouring it in.

In the box below, draw a happy situation or use a colour to symbolise happiness.

Worksheet 6 The present

Think of someone you love and make a drawing of that person:

If that person gave you a present what would your behavioural response be? - what would you do?

_____

how would you feel?

_____

what would you say?

_____

what would be two inappropriate responses?

_____

_____

Worksheet 7 Liking and smiling

Tell some one what you like about them.

Ask some one to explain how she or he feels when smiling; listen to the answer.

Either draw yourself smiling or a shape that represents joy to you:

Sheet A

Belinda gets help.

Sheet B

Sheet C

Sheet D

Belinda's Mummy makes an appointment for her to see someone to help her.

Sheet E

Sheet F

Sheet G

Sheet H

While Belinda is with Yoko, Kitty goes to sleep and happily dreams.

Sheet J

Sheet K

Sheet L

Sheet M

Sheet O

Sheet P

Sheet Q

Sheet R

Sheet S

 My name is ...

 I am   years old.

 My friend's name is ...

 My teacher's name is ...

 My favourite drink is ...

 My favourite food is ...

 My favourite game is ...

 I like ...

 When I grow up I want to be a ...

Afterword

Please note that if you are interested in contributing to the collection of evidence which teaching emotional literacy can be based on, then please send copies of your work to me, the author, care of the publisher. It is understood that if you do so, you agree to the contents you send being included in any future publication, which you will be acknowledged for.

References

Apter, T. (1997) The Confident Child New York, London, Norton.

Baker, P. (1998) Here's Health magazine March 20-22.

Berne, E. (1964) Games people play - The psychology of human relationships, New York: Grove Press.

Berne, E. (1970) Sex in human loving, New York: Simon and Schuster.

Brady, R., Bacon, J. and Ryves, D. (2000) A case study illustrating potential adverse impact in two popular psychometric ability tests Selection Development Review 16 (4) 10-15.

Brown, J. (1998) Large-scale health promotion stress workshops: promotion and client response. Brighton 1998 British Psychological Society annual conference, unpublished paper.

Chopra, D. (1993) Ageless Body Timeless Mind London, Rider.

Cole, T. (1998) Peer support new beginnings in Japan Peer support networker Issue 9, 6-7.

Cowie, H. (1998) Editorial; Peer support networker Issue 9, 1.

Dixon, R. (1998) Interventions across Europe to combat bullying ; A personal view; Peer support networker Issue 9, 3-4.

Goleman, D. (1995 1st ed.) Emotional Intelligence New York, Bantam.

Goleman, D. (1996 2nd ed.) Emotional Intelligence London, Bloomsbury.

Gottman, J. (1998) The Heart of Parenting London, Bloomsbury.

Grant, W.T. (1992) Consortium on the School-Based Promotion of Social Competence, Drug and Alcohol Prevention Curricula; in Hawkins, J.D. et al (1992) 'Communities that Care' San Francisco, Josey-Bass.

Gross, J; Kaplan, L; Gurner, A; Jackson, S; Maines, B; Clemson, S; Walker, S; Sidebottom, D; Hill, J; Sanday, H; Marson, P; Wardle, C. and Stinchcombe, V. (2000) <u>The emotional literacy hour</u> Bristol: Lucky Duck Publishing Ltd..

Jacobs, A. (1973) <u>TA and psychodrama</u>. In M. James (Ed.). Techniques in transactional analysis for psychotherapists and counsellors (239-249) Reading MA: Addison-Wesley.

James, M. (1981) <u>Breaking Free</u> Reading MA: Addison-Wesley.

Makin, P. and Ruitenbeck, D.V. (1998) <u>The psychological contract as a close relationship</u>. Brighton 1998 British Psychological Society annual conference, unpublished paper.

Martin, P. (1998) <u>The psychological contract as a close relationship</u> Brighton, 1998 British Psychological Society annual conference, unpublished paper.

McGrellis, S., Thomas, R., Holland, J., Henderson, S. and Sharpe. S. (1998) <u>Hoping for heaven: fearing exclusion; the location of young people's fears in time and place</u>. Brighton 1998 British Psychological Society annual conference, unpublished paper.

Mortimer, H. (1998) <u>Personal and social development</u> Scholastic Limited; in Rudd, B. 1998 Talking is for Kids Bristol, Lucky Duck Publishing Ltd.

Piaget, J. (1929) <u>The child's conception of the world</u> New York, Harcourt, Brace and World.

Piaget, J. (1963) <u>The origins of intelligence in children</u> New York, Norton.

Piaget, J. (1951) <u>Play, dreams and imitation in childhood</u> London, Routledge.

Piaget, J. (1932) <u>The moral judgement of the child</u> New York, Harcourt, Brace and World.

Piaget, J. (1952) <u>The child's conception of number</u> London, Routledge and Kegan.

Robinson, G. and Maines, B. (1998) Circle time resources Bristol, Lucky Duck Publishing Ltd.

Rudd, B. (1998) Talking is for Kids – Emotional Literacy for Infant School Children Bristol, Lucky Duck Publishing.

Schilling, D. (1996) Emotional Intelligence Level 1 Toronto, California, Innerchoice Publishing.

Simons, J. (1998) Paradoxes in learning and teaching Brighton, 1998 British Psychological Society annual conference, unpublished paper.

Steiner, C. (1996) Emotional literacy training: The application of transactional analysis to the study of emotions; in Transactional Analysis Journal 26 (1) 31-38.

Stacey, H., Robinson, P. (1997) Lets Mediate Bristol, Lucky Duck Publishing Ltd.

Stacey, H. (2001) Peer mediation training for young people Bristol, Lucky Duck Publishing Ltd.

Swallow, B. and Romick, R. (1998) Towards the millennium: young people's values, beliefs and thoughts Brighton, 1998 British Psychological Society annual conference, unpublished paper.

Wallace, F. (1998) What else can I do with you? Bristol, Lucky Duck Publishing Ltd.

Appendix 1

List of useful resources

i <u>Body Mind Update</u>: This is a much needed publication which informs the lay person of the latest research on the links between body and mind. It also offers practical tips on being healthier in mind and body. Send a note, with a stamped self addressed envelope, stating what you would like, to Body Mind Update, PO Box 67, Uckfield, TN22 3DE.

ii <u>British Chiropractic Association</u>: This professional body has a list of all registered doctors of chiropractic. These chiropractors can check a child's structural alignment, since they specialise in muscular-skeletal problems. It is a little known fact that they are officially recognised as primary care practitioners. It is possible for a child to be experiencing difficulties because of a structural problem, as opposed to a purely psychological one. To find your closest qualified doctor of chiropractic look for the BCA box in your local Yellow Pages telephone directory.

iii <u>Counsellor's Guild (CG)</u>: If you are interested in developing the three core qualities of empathy (compassion), congruence (honesty) and unconditional positive regard (acceptance), then you can benefit from taking a counselling skills course. An excellent one is Co1, run by CG. You can obtain a prospectus from P.O. Box 67, Uckfield, TN22 3DE.

iv <u>Educating Children With Special Needs</u>: The title of this book explains succinctly what it is about. The authors are Ashman, A. and Elkins, J. it was published in 1990 and can be obtained from Prentice Hall in London.

v <u>EQ Game</u>: This co-operative card game for ages 4 years to adult is excellent for facilitating emotional intelligence in individuals; it uses a variety of cards dealing with emotion, speech and action (relating to the crucial areas of affect, cognition and behaviour). The game can be obtained from: Body Mind Update, PO Box 67, Uckfield, TN22 3DE.

vi <u>Feelings, Stories for Assembly and P.S.E.</u>: This book, published in 1994 by Southgate Publishers Limited and written by G. Apsland, offers a selection of fifteen stories which focus on issues that deal with friendship, responsibility and fairness. The book is aimed at junior schools.

vii Grief Game: This board game can be usefully played with any one who is suffering from bereavement. It can be purchased from Jessica Kingsley Press in London.

viii Talking is for Kids: A very useful book on emotional literacy for children aged from four to eight years, by Betty K. Rudd. This can be purchased from Lucky Duck Publishing Ltd. in Bristol, Tel: 0117 973 2881 Fax: 0117 973 1707.

ix The Counsellor's Basics: This is a short handbook which describes the qualities of empathy, congruence and unconditional positive regard, clearly and simply. It can not only be read from cover to cover, but it can also be used as a basic reference book on active listening. Order a copy from PO Box 67, Uckfield, TN22 3DE.

x The Emotional Literacy Hour: This is a video by Luck Duck with an accompanying book. It demonstrates a variety of activities to develop emotional literacy in nursery, primary and secondary schools. Please contact Lucky Duck if you would like a copy. You can either telephone 0117 973 2881 or write to 3 Thorndale Mews, Clifton, Bristol, BS8 2HX.

Lucky Duck has a wide range of materials on emotional development. Please contact them for their latest catalogue or visit their web page: www.luckyduck.co.uk

Appendix 2 on pages 80 & 81

The emotional curriculum – a developmental progression.

Developed by Bristol Teachers and Psychologists
Reprinted from 'The Emotional Literacy Hour' with permission of Lucky Duck Publishing Ltd.

The emotional curriculum – a developmental progression.

Talking About Feelings	Listening Skills	Self Awareness	Managing Feelings	Empathy	Goal-Setting and Planning – Problem Solving and Decision Making
Non-verbal expression of feelings – crying, laughing.	Earliest signals – eye contact, attention, turn head.	Experiencing pleasure, discomfort or pain.			Goals are immediate and waiting impossible.
Expressing need "want", desire "no".	Following simple instruction.	Having sad, cross, happy feelings.		Simple reflex response to others emotions eg: smile at another's pleasure, cry if see something hurt.	Beginning to be aware of a time scale beyond the here and now, and to be able to predict events.
Acknowledging "I feel sad," "I feel happy" to adult prompt.	Listening to story – extended attention.			Simple acts based on what would make themselves better eg: giving another child their comfort object to hold.	Can set short-term goals with adult help (eg: High Scope).
	Turn taking in conversation.		Knowing that it is OK to have both positive and negative feelings.	Early sharing (I will share because they have not got any).	Can imagine good things to come and tolerate waiting/ turntaking.
Acknowledging more complex feelings after adult prompting.	Can encourage other person to talk and use eye contact, body language etc.				Can set and describe short term goals without help.
Being able to separate the facts of an event (fight etc) from the feelings.	Listen to story, answer questions about content.	Thinking about feelings.	Developing ways of managing your own feelings eg: asking for help, saying how you feel.	Simple perspective taking eg: answering questions about a story – "How do you think Brown Bear is feeling?"	Can set and describe longer term goals, and begin to make informed choices between "now" and "later".
Recognising and describing own feelings in specific situations. Developing emotional vocabulary for describing own feelings (eg: I feel worried, scared, pleased) and for gradations of feelings (a bit scared, very scared).			Being able to receive and respond to others' strong emotions.		Can generate alternative solutions to social/ interpersonal problems and begin to identify consequence of doing x, y, or z.

Using vocabulary of more subtle emotions eg: embarrassment, shame, anxiety, jealousy. Knowing when it is appropriate to talk about feelings and when it is not.	Reflecting back feelings/content of spoken information. Inferring meaning, predicting, hypothising. Reflecting back in simple ways the unspoken feelings behind what another person is saying.	Understanding the natural and normal range of feelings experienced after major event such as bereavement/loss.	Developing more complex way of managing feelings, eg: assertiveness, visualisation, relaxation, changing the way you internally talk to yourself and perceive/label events.	Can take responsibility for own actions and understand their effects on others. Can plan intermediate steps towards a goal. Can identify a range of solutions to social/interpersonal problems, examine the probable consequences of each, and make a choice on the basis of this evaluation.
Using "I messages" (When you do x I feel y, and the consequence are z) to verbalise feelings without blame and to give positive strokes to others.	Using "You feel ... because" when listening. Not being afraid of silence. Being able to follow/summarise content and feeling of what others have said.	Understanding the relationship between thoughts, feeling and actions. Knowing if a thought or feeling is ruling a decision, and being able to identify that thought or that feeling.	More complex clue reading to deduce others' feelings - simple feelings of pleasure, anger, sadness. Can pick up others very subtle emotions - embarrassment, jealousy, shame etc.	Review choices made to see if they worked out. Able to postpone gratification for the sake of others - and work to intrinsic goals.
			Multiple perspective taking - seeing everybody's side of things. Can maintain empathy beyond the here and now. Ability to empathise in relation to imagined situations outside own experience.	
Using conflict management skills.	Using conflict management skills.	Knowing whether a feeling/behaviour is coming from an internal child, adult or parent position.	Ability to manage and channel empathy; maintain boundary between self and others; choose whether or not to make a response as a result of empathic feelings.	